Original title:
The Joy of Silent Nights

Copyright © 2024 Creative Arts Management OÜ
All rights reserved.

Author: Julian Montgomery
ISBN HARDBACK: 978-9916-94-026-6
ISBN PAPERBACK: 978-9916-94-027-3

Ambiance of the Night Breeze

The crickets chirp a silly tune,
As if they danced beneath the moon.
A raccoon steals my midnight snack,
And then he winks, I try to act.

A breeze that tickles, makes me laugh,
As shadows play a moonlit half.
The stars giggle in their glow,
As autumn leaves begin to blow.

The Softness of Night's Canvas

The night sky wears a velvet dress,
With twinkling gems, it's quite a mess.
I trip on clouds that float so free,
While owls hoot out their melody.

A silly dog chases a tail,
As fireflies weave a glowing trail.
Each twinkle brightens my late night,
It's a comedy of cosmic light.

Soft Sighs of the Moon

The moon winks down with a cheeky grin,
While we all snicker at the silly spin.
A lone cat meows like it's an opera,
Making midnight feel like a grand drama.

A breeze whispers secrets, oh so absurd,
As I quietly ponder, slightly disturbed.
With every hush, the laughter spreads,
As sleepy dreams dance in my head.

Ethereal Embrace of Dusk

Dusk tiptoes in, with a playful flair,
Painting shadows with mischievous care.
The stars peek out with a blush of glee,
It's a cosmic circus, just for me.

The crickets hold a nightly show,
While sleepy deer put on a toe.
With chuckles lingering in the air,
Night's gentle laughter is everywhere.

A Hush Over the World

When crickets hold orchestra's grace,
And moths dance like they own the place.
A cat tiptoes on a midnight spree,
While I search for snacks, oh woe is me!

The clock strikes twelve, I hear it chime,
Who knew silence could be so sublime?
The fridge hums softly, my secret pal,
As I raid it like a midnight gal!

The Art of Silent Reverie

Stars chat quietly, what do they say?
Maybe gossip about cats at play.
Whispers of dreams drift on the breeze,
While my neighbor snores loud as a sneeze.

I tiptoe past the sleeping dog,
Who dreams of chasing a digital frog.
Moonlight's laughter spills on the ground,
As I stumble softly, without a sound.

Nightfall's Tender Secrets

Bats swoop low with a wink and a nod,
While I sip my cocoa, feeling quite odd.
The shadows plot with a mischievous grin,
As the tired world begins to spin.

A sloth on a branch, taking its time,
Who knew that laziness could feel so prime?
The glow of the moon brings a giggle delight,
As I trip over shoes in the soft night light.

Embracing Twilight's Calm

The world slows down with a silly sigh,
While fireflies join in, oh my, oh my!
A raccoon prances with trash bag flair,
In this funny theater, nothing's a scare.

My teddy bear whispers some late-night puns,
While the sock drawer offers its silly runs.
In stillness, we gather, with laughter and glee,
For even the night can share its spree!

Ballet of Shadows and Stars

Under the moon, shadows play tricks,
Dancing around, like quirky little picks.
Squirrels in pajamas, birds in ballet,
Who knew the night could be such a sway?

Stars are winking, gossiping bright,
Whispering secrets, keeping it light.
A cat in a tux, a dog in a tie,
Critiquing the moon, oh my, oh my!

Tranquil Moments Unveiled

In the still, the fridge hums a tune,
As a mouse in a hat plots to swoon.
Under the blanket, popcorn in hand,
Just me and my dreams, isn't it grand?

The clock gives a yawn, it's tired of ticks,
While the dog starts to plot daring tricks.
A dance of the shadows upon the wall,
Making me giggle, oh what a ball!

Night's Gentle Lullaby

Crickets compose with their offbeat cheer,
As I sip cocoa and silence draws near.
A raccoon declares it's his time to shine,
With hiccups and twirls, our own little shrine.

The stars in their pajamas glow like a flare,
While I contemplate if I should snack or spare.
A comet zooms by, rides on a whim,
Singing a tune, just a bit out of trim!

Hushed Symphony of the Cosmos

Galaxies giggle in the velvet sky,
While I try to stir, fighting a sigh.
The sofa summons, with a melody sweet,
With cushions that promise a night of retreat.

In the background, the crickets compete,
For the loudest of laughs, a rhythmic feat.
Moonbeams in tutus waltz 'round the floor,
In this silent hush, it's a delightful lore.

A Palette of Evening Serenity

Stars twinkle like a cheeky light,
While crickets tap dance through the night.
The moon wears shades of cheesy glee,
As owls hoot jokes, just for me.

The wind chuckles, whispers so sly,
As fireflies flicker, oh my! oh my!
A breeze plays tag with sleepy trees,
While dreams snooze, sipping tea with ease.

In this calm, giggles softly creep,
While shadows gather, plotting to leap.
A world that's hushed, yet full of cheer,
Where laughter bubbles, crystal clear.

So here's to nights that gently tease,
Where even silence dances with ease.
In a palette of soft, silvery hues,
Life paints joy in every snooze.

The Floating Hush of Moonlight

In the stillness, whispers glide,
As moonbeams play, oh, what a ride!
With giggles of frogs in a pond's embrace,
And stars pulling pranks in their glowing space.

Crickets crack jokes, and they sing,
While owls juggle all their bling.
The night air tickles with frothy delight,
As shadows muse, avoiding the light.

The breeze wears a hat, so dapper and bright,
Chasing the twinkling light out of sight.
As thoughts wander, they secretly flirt,
With all the chuckles, it's hard not to smirk.

So let's toast to this sneaky affair,
Where silence and laughter are quite the pair.
In a floating hush, where giggles ignite,
The moon's gentle smirk keeps the night light.

Night's Choreography of Stillness

In the dark, a ballet begins,
Where shadows glide, and laughter spins.
With stars as dancers on a stage so grand,
Performing silly moves at night's command.

The crickets chirp a rhythm divine,
While fireflies twirl in a sparkling line.
Owls pull pranks, with a wink and a hoot,
In this twilight play, where silliness is cute.

Trees sway softly, a whimsical wave,
As the night wears costumes, bold and brave.
The gentle breeze joins in the fun,
Flinging giggles, one by one.

So here's to the dance of evening's tale,
Where silence is quirky, and peace won't fail.
In night's choreography, we take delight,
As laughter pirouettes into the night.

Navigating Through the Stars' Stillness

Under the moon's sleepy glare,
My cat plots schemes in the air.
Stars twinkle like distant glee,
While I sip tea and let it be.

Crickets chirp their nightly tune,
Making plans for a dance at noon.
The owl hoots like it's half asleep,
As I count wishes in a heap.

A raccoon steals my midnight snack,
With stealth that leaves me quite slack.
"Hey!" I shout, but he's not fazed,
In his own world, he's truly glazed.

I chuckle at the night's parade,
While dreams and snacks seem to evade.
A silent night, a playful dream,
With chaos lurking in moonbeams.

The Beauty of Unbroken Silence

In the hush, my thoughts ride high,
A sneaky whisper from the pie.
Laughter floats through evening mist,
As I recall each tasty twist.

Neighbors' snores form a symphony,
A loud encore—so heavenly!
Dogs growl softly in their sleep,
A night parade I'd like to keep.

Blankets rustle, dreams run wild,
While moon's light plays like a child.
Amidst this calm, I laugh and sigh,
Realizing peace can make us fly.

Yet in the towards-becoming gust,
With eyelids heavy, I adjust.
For in quiet, my dreams ignite,
A world where silliness takes flight.

Glimmers of Calm After Dark

The clock strikes twelve, I'm wide awake,
Wondering if rats will bake a cake.
Outside, the shadows seem to creep,
Perhaps they're planning a midnight leap.

Dust bunnies hold a wild dance,
In my corner, they take a chance.
I join in with a little spin,
Imagining the chaos that is within.

A ghostly wind gives a playful shove,
As I mumble 'tis all in love.
The glow from stars plays hide and seek,
I laugh aloud—who needs to speak?

In silence, the laughter flows,
With tales only the night knows.
I'll giggle through the rest of this spree,
As the night wraps its arms around me.

The Quiet Reverie

In soft shadows, I take a seat,
With dreams that dance on laughter's beat.
The dog snores loud—night's comic show,
While trees sway gently, putting on a glow.

My socks debate a daring steal,
A funny drama, oh what a deal!
Crickets are cast in a nightly plight,
As the stars just chuckle at their flight.

Each second, a giggle finds its way,
To tickle my heart, come what may.
As the night unfurls its quiet charm,
I sit back, wrapped in its warm, soft balm.

So here I scribe this silly tale,
Where unbroken peace does prevail.
In laughter and dreams, I take my flight,
Navigating joy in the quiet night.

The Silence that Sings

In the stillness, whispers play,
Like crickets jamming, hip-hip-hooray!
The moon giggles down from the sky,
While sleepy owls give their best try.

Laughter floats on the midnight breeze,
Mice tap dance under the trees.
Stars in pajamas twinkle and blink,
As the universe takes a wink.

In corners, shadows throw a show,
Where gigglebugs gather in a row.
Who knew silence could be so loud?
With invisible friends, I'm feeling proud.

The night hums with a quirky tune,
As cats karaoke beneath the moon.
Every star a tiny fan club's cheer,
In our secret, hilarious, night-time sphere.

Nocturnal Reflections

In dreams, we ride on fluffy clouds,
Wearing pajamas, feeling proud.
While pillows plot, they giggle away,
Spreading laughter till break of day.

The stars wink with a goofy style,
As crickets share jokes all the while.
The trees sway in a rhythmic sway,
To a tune that seems to say, 'Stay!'

Moonlight paints shadows with glee,
Imaginary friends toast with tea.
In the dark, silliness takes flight,
As we celebrate this comical night.

Reflections dance in the pond so bright,
Where frogs croak out their very best bite.
A night where laughter reigns supreme,
In our dreams, we craft a funny theme.

Traces of Stardust in the Air

Underneath the cosmic quilt,
We find traces of joy that's built.
With a pinch of stardust, we dance and twirl,
As sleepy towns begin to swirl.

Fireflies string lights in the dark,
While the moon sips cocoa in its park.
Whispers exchange like goodnight winks,
Between those who dream and the pens that ink.

Laughter trails like a comet's tail,
As night critters spin a funny tale.
Every rustle, a chuckle's grin,
In the patchwork sky, where tales begin.

With each step, the night hums fun,
Tickle the stars for a giggle run.
It's a circus of dreams alight,
In the canvas of the twilight night.

The Magic of Gentle Breezes

The gentle breeze fluffs up my hair,
It whispers secrets with utmost care.
A tickle here, a nudge right there,
Turns the night into magical flair.

Dancing leaves make a merry sound,
While the grass plays the world's best round.
A chorus of murmurs fills the air,
As night critters strut without a care.

With every gust, the giggles rise,
As shadows prance beneath the skies.
The cool night air hums out loud,
Knocking socks off the sleepy crowd.

The moon, so cheeky, throws a glance,
As the world around begins to dance.
In the magic of breezes soft and light,
We find our smiles under the starlit night.

Beneath the Velvet Sky

Under a sky so deep and blue,
Even the owls are dozing too.
The stars are winking, having a laugh,
While crickets form a nighttime staff.

Beneath the velvet, all is still,
Not a sound, not a single thrill.
A snail jogs by, oh what a sight,
Winning the race with all his might!

Moonbeams tickle the tree limbs high,
As squirrels plot to steal the pie.
A cat joins in on the midnight spree,
Chasing shadows, wild and free.

In the library of the night,
Books that whisper, time takes flight.
Dreams pirouette on velvet beams,
Life is funnier than it seems.

Dreams in the Quiet Hours

When the clock strikes twelve, it's time to play,
The midnight mouse plays jazz ballet.
The stars are clapping, in their own way,
As dreams frolic, hip-hip-hooray!

A pillow fights back, soft and plump,
While sleepyheads inside it thump.
They giggle in whispers, soft as frost,
Counting sheep? Oh, they're all lost!

An old teddy bear hums a tune,
Under a sleepy, quarter moon.
With a wink and a nod, they reminisce,
About a time they snatched a kiss.

The corner lamp does a silly dance,
As shadows twirl in a dreamy trance.
In the quiet hours, laughter flies,
While mischief learns to improvise.

Lullabies of the Night

A wind that whispers through the trees,
Plays tag with leaves, as it teases.
Squirrels yawn and stretch their tails,
Plotting their next nutty tales.

The moonlight drips like melting cheese,
Over rooftops with the greatest ease.
Under blankets, all snug and tight,
Snore choirs harmonize the night.

A soft-spoken toad croaks out of tune,
While fireflies join as they swoon.
A dance-off starts among the bugs,
With fancy footwork, and giant shrugs!

In these lullabies, dreams tickle and tease,
As kittens pounce and attempt to please.
The night is silly, with giggles so bright,
In the lull of dark, we find pure delight.

Stars' Gentle Murmurs

Stars chatter softly, gossiping bright,
About all the silliness of the night.
A raccoon tries to set a record,
For stealing snacks—he's such a nerd!

A flurry of laughter fills the air,
As owls play poker without a care.
While frogs in tuxedos croon their songs,
The night holds magic, where all belongs.

A playful breeze gives strands a swirl,
As pajamas twirl in a sleepy whirl.
Bouncing in dreams, oh what a sight,
Finding joy in the heart of night.

With every murmur, the stars confide,
In whispers bright, the laughter will bide.
In this symphony of sleepy cheer,
The world finds chuckles, year after year.

The Subtle Dance of Night's Breath

In the quiet, shadows sway,
A sock found on the floor, hooray!
Cats plotting schemes in moonlit beams,
While I trip over dreams, it seems.

The creaks of wood, a ghostly tune,
Telling tales of spoons gone soon.
Midnight snacks, a stealthy feast,
Peanut butter? Oh, the least!

Chairs that groan with every crawl,
I wonder if they'll last through all.
Yet in this calm, delight's found,
In the quirky noises all around.

So here's to nights, both strange and light,
Where laughter bubbles through the night.
In the escapades of moonlit fun,
I rise to greet the rising sun!

Ephemeral Light in Dark Corners

A flicker from the fridge draws near,
Like a lighthouse, sweet and clear.
I steal a snack, try not to wake,
The slumbering beast, my sleeping flake.

Beneath the stars, the couch starts to hum,
Is that my thoughts? Or just some gum?
Mismatched socks seem to conspire,
Beneath the pillows, they conspire.

Each chuckle hides in nighttime's cloak,
As spoons engage in chatty yoke.
The shadows giggle, a secret fight,
My snacks are gone by morning light!

In every nook, laughter's spread,
Whispers of mischief in my head.
With each blink, the night unfolds,
Hilarious tales yet to be told!

Emotions Beneath Still Sheets

Under covers, a ruckus brews,
Pillow forts and mystery clues.
Emotions wrestle, toss and turn,
For midnight snacks we surely yearn.

With every rustle, giggles bloom,
As blankets become a cozy room.
A battle fought with a feathered tease,
Against sleepyheads, I take my ease.

Thoughts of dragons in the mist,
What a time to play a prank or twist!
Dreams are nudged by tapping feet,
Imaginary snacks fairies' treat.

So let the night be filled with cheer,
As laughter dances, sharp and clear.
With whispers shared and silences bold,
Each pillow fort cements the gold!

Whispers in the Dark

Whispers glide like playful winds,
Secrets shared where mischief begins.
The moon's a witness to all my schemes,
As laughter tickles the edges of dreams.

Sneaking snacks like stealthy ninjas,
While the cat gives me judgmental twinges.
In the stillness, shadows play,
Each creaky floor a cheeky ballet.

Ghosts of giggles float around,
Echoes of joy in silence found.
So let the clock strike one or two,
With every whisper, it's a hullabaloo!

As dawn approaches, we part with grace,
Dreams still dancing, we quicken our pace.
In the hush of night, we lose track of time,
Crafting memories, in rhythm and rhyme!

Moonbeams on Whispering Trees

Moonlight dances on the leaves,
Squirrels plotting mischief reprieves.
Owls hoot jokes to feathered friends,
Nature's laughter never ends.

Crickets chirp in secret glee,
While shadows waltz around the tree.
A raccoon munches on a snack,
And giggles echo down the track.

A breeze teases the night so sweet,
As fireflies showcase their twinkling feat.
Every rustle brings a sigh,
Under the gaze of the twinkling high.

Moonlit pranks and stealthy shows,
Even the fox in a mask knows.
In the stillness, laughter thrives,
With nighttime fun, the world arrives.

The Quietude of Dreamscapes

In slumber's grip, the whispers play,
A pillow fight breaks the calm array.
Pajamas twist in a silly flurry,
As dreams and giggles start to hurry.

Teddy bears plot their midnight scheme,
To steal the spotlight, or so they dream.
Under covers, tickles abound,
In this serenade, joy is found.

Stars peek in with a knowing grin,
As night owls boast about their win.
The moon rolls eyes at the ruckus made,
While sleepyheads in laughter fade.

The dreamscape echoes their delight,
In the stillness, everything seems right.
A cocoon of chuckles softly spins,
As sleepy time begins and wins.

Still Moments Beneath the Stars

Beneath the twinkle, shadows lark,
A squirrel plans a bold remark.
Moonlit beams on houses glow,
As laughter floats on breezes slow.

A gentle snore breaks the night,
As neighbors gossip without fright.
A dog barks softly at a cat,
In their twilit, comical spat.

Whispers dance like dandelion seeds,
Nature's humor plants its deeds.
Fireflies play hide and seek,
In the glow, their secrets peek.

Laughter's echo fills the air,
Under the charm of the midnight care.
With silly stories shared by all,
The night wraps them in its shawl.

Soft Footfalls of the Night

Soft footsteps tiptoe through the whirls,
As hedgehogs strut in their huffy twirls.
Bunnies hop as if on cue,
To share their tales of nightly dew.

Mice gather round, their giggles sly,
Plotting pranks under the starry sky.
Every rustle brings a cheer,
As laughter echoes far and near.

The world in stillness hums a tune,
While whispers chase the silver moon.
A fox investigates with glee,
At the antics of his woodland spree.

A night adorned with silly sights,
Exuberant joy in the blink of lights.
With soft footfalls echoing bright,
The laughter blooms under starlit light.

Solitude's Soft Glow

In the quiet of dusk, I sip my tea,
My cat looks at me like I'm a spree.
The fridge hums a tune, so offbeat and loud,
I dance in my socks, feeling quite proud.

The stars peek above, in their twinkly way,
I trip on my rug, as I sway and sway.
The neighbors are snoring, their dreams take flight,
While I bust a move in the low moonlight.

Mellow Shadows at Dusk

Shadows creep in, like a secret friend,
I laugh at my shadow, it won't even bend.
The toaster pops up, it's toast time hooray,
But it lands on the floor, just to spoil my play.

A spider's web weaves, a glistening thread,
I whisper to it, 'Now, please don't be dead.'
The fridge sings a tune, while the clock tick-tocks,
I join in the chorus, with wobbly knocks.

Peace Wrapped in Darkness

In darkness I linger, my snack is a feat,
Chips crinkle loudly, oh what a treat!
I pause and I listen, the night holds its breath,
While visions of nachos dance close to death.

The couch casts its spell, so cozy and warm,
But oh, what's that smell? Is it me or the charm?
The night may be quiet, but I still can hear,
The laughter of dreams, whispering near.

A Serenade of Crickets

Crickets are singing, a comical choir,
Their off-tune croaking, a wild, funny fire.
I clap to the rhythm, in the soft moon's glow,
While fireflies twinkle like stars on the show.

The trees start to sway, they join in the cheer,
But I trip on a root, 'Oh dear, never fear!'
The night stretches wide, with giggles and dreams,
And all my odd antics are just what it seems.

Night's Gentle Whispers

Stars giggle in the sky,
Winking at my sleepy eye.
Cats plot in the moonlight,
While mice prepare for their flight.

Crickets sing their offbeat tunes,
Dancing 'neath the chubby moons.
Owls wear spectacles and read,
As squirrels plan a midnight feed.

Breezes tickle sleepy ears,
Pillow fights with fluff and cheers.
Lampshades nod, the clock does yawn,
As daytime dreams become a con.

Even shadows wear a grin,
As night begins a cheeky spin.
Whispers weave through trees and rooms,
In this realm, only laughter blooms.

Soft Echoes of the Universe

Starlight weaves a quirky tale,
Of a snail who rode a whale.
Planets spin in jolly jest,
Leaving rabbits quite impressed.

Nebulae float with twinkling glee,
While space dust giggles endlessly.
Chasing comets, kites they fly,
In the backdrop of the night sky.

Meteor showers drop like tricks,
Shooting stars and cosmic flicks.
Black holes dance a silly jig,
While constellations start to dig.

Galaxies draw silly maps,
Of how to avoid cosmic naps.
In this humor-filled expanse,
Even silence finds a chance.

The Peaceful Pulse of Night

In the stillness, whispers play,
Balloons drift in a floaty sway.
Chairs gossip with furniture friends,
While time giggles and never ends.

Bats wear capes in shadowed flight,
As deep yawn echoes through the night.
Moonbeams tease with soft caress,
Tickling drowsy dreams, no less.

Lamps fidget, casting light-hugs,
Cats stretch in their night-time plugs.
Even socks share tales of friends,
Lurking under beds, it never ends.

With crickets kicking off the vibe,
Nighttime's a merry jive describe.
Mirth hides soft in every sound,
As joy, in silence, can be found.

Serenity in the Absence of Sound

Without a word, the night unfurls,
Where giggling shadows spin and twirl.
The air is thick with secret sighs,
As sleep begins to close its eyes.

The fridge hums a silly song,
While dreams march in a silly throng.
Blankets snicker, soft and warm,
As the night wraps in cozy charm.

Bees in dreams buzz with delight,
In slumber's grasp, all feels just right.
The tick of clocks can't stop the fun,
As night's escapades have just begun.

So here we lie, in blissful hush,
Welcomed by the night's soft rush.
Smiles grow wide in the quiet glow,
As laughter dances, soft and slow.

Twilight Twilight's Gentle Caress

As shadows stretch and yawning grows,
The cats start scheming, striking poses.
They prance and pounce without a care,
While humans stumble, unaware.

A fridge door creaks, snacks lay in wait,
Mmm, chips and dips, oh what a fate!
The silence thick, it's hard to hear,
A crunch resounds, but who is near?

Outside, owls hoot, a wise old crew,
While crickets chirp a nightly tune.
The harried day seems far away,
Yet here we giggle, come what may.

In twilight's grasp, absurdities reign,
Intentionally misplaced, the dog's insane.
With sock in mouth, he takes a dash,
Making midnight mischief, quite a smash!

Under the Silver Gaze

Moonbeams dance on distant ground,
While raccoons plot without a sound.
They sneak through trash, it's quite absurd,
Their laughter lost, but how it's heard!

A ghostly cat takes center stage,
With whiskers long and full of rage.
She leaps, she bounds, a fierce ballet,
While humans laugh, in sheer dismay.

The clock chimes softly, hours unwind,
As thoughts grow sillier, unconfined.
Whispers fly like paper planes,
Silly stories, teasing refrains.

Under bright stars, laughter swirls,
As friendship blooms and mischief twirls.
In shadows deep, the giggles rise,
Sharing secrets under the skies!

The Quietude of Time

In evening's hush, a ponderous sigh,
While socks go missing, oh my, oh my!
The toaster pops, a phantom bite,
As crumbs do dance in ghostly light.

Mismatched shoes in a tangled heap,
Who knew that silence could be so cheap?
The dog dreams deep, a peaceful sight,
While cats engage in feline fights.

A cup of tea and a scrabble word,
The laughter rings out, oh, how absurd!
Fingers fumbling, words misplaced,
We giggle hard, our thoughts embraced.

In quiet hours, antics unfold,
Stories shared, both new and old.
Together we wander through this maze,
In silent nights, we lose our ways!

Mellow Tones of Evening Air

The sun dips low, a warm retreat,
Where ants parade in fine deceit.
They march in line with no parade,
Yet somehow manage, late night's charade.

A chair creaks loud, oh what a sound,
The cat shoots up, her feet unbound.
As she surveys her noble realm,
It's just a sock that's at the helm.

Outside the breeze starts to play,
As neighbors shout, they've lost their way.
In silent jest, we tease and laugh,
At all the chaos on our path.

As night unfolds, dreams take flight,
With laughter shared till morning light.
Amidst the calm, the funny prevails,
In mellow tones, our joy unveils!

Moonbeams and Silenced Thoughts

When moonbeams tease the sleepy town,
Cats compete, wearing their best frown.
Whispers dance in the starry air,
While owls hoot, without a care.

A pizza slice dreams on the floor,
Squeaky shoes from the neighbor's door.
The clock ticks loudly, but who gives a hoot?
Life's funniest jokes, all lend a toot!

A squirrel steals the neighbor's hat,
Bragging rights to a midnight chat.
Pajamas parade with mismatched flair,
As giggles echo from everywhere!

In quirky shadows, shadows play,
Candles flicker in a silly ballet.
With silly dreams that softly collide,
The night laughs quietly, side by side.

Night's Gentle Soliloquy

In a world where snoring takes the lead,
Dreamers plot with some midnight greed.
Teddy bears hold conferences at play,
While socks embark on a getaway.

Buzzy bugs join in a moonlit dance,
Curious creaks give night a chance.
The fridge hums along with a soothing tune,
As chubby raccoons pop up to swoon.

Pillow fights spark a giggle storm,
With whispers that challenge the quiet norm.
Under comforters, dreams take flight,
As laughter spills into the night.

So grab your dreams and keep it light,
Under stars, we'll giggle till first light.
Each tale spun in a delicious weave,
For nighttime mischief, we never grieve.

The Coziness of Midnight Hues

Fluffy blankets share secrets deep,
While chilly drafts invite us to peep.
Cookies crumble in a crumbly parade,
As the clock's chimes start to invade.

Pajamas dance with socks askew,
Jumping jacks in the midnight blue.
Mismatched mittens, so proud to be,
In this cozy land of make-believe.

Laughter spills from the kitchen's gate,
As playful memories eagerly await.
With hot cocoa that tickles the tongue,
We sing silly songs that we've just sprung.

So let's delight in this splendid show,
Where moonlight and giggles freely flow.
A sprinkle of fun, a dash of grace,
In the cozy arms of this silly space.

Reflections in Limbo

In the spirit of the dreaming hour,
The truth is masked by the moon's soft power.
Dishes stack up, but who really cares?
Midnight snacks lend the evening flair.

Toothpaste battles, who could have guessed?
With foam-fueled giggles, we're all blessed.
The toaster pops, it's a soft explosion,
As chaos whispers of our sweet devotion.

Giddy thoughts on the pillow's edge,
Our minds are free to dance and pledge.
Chasing shadows that twirl and spin,
As the world outside falls quietly in.

So let's toast to stars that brightly joke,
This world of whimsy, where fun's bespoke.
We slumber lightly in a wondrous glow,
Where hilarity blooms and laughter flows.

Celestial Murmurs

Under the sleepy moon's beam,
Whispers float in a cosmic dream.
Stars giggle like kids at play,
While crickets join in the cabaret.

The owls hoot their thoughts on mice,
While night slips by oh-so-nice.
A fox twirls in the moon's embrace,
As if winning a dance-off in space.

Soft shadows shoo away the light,
While slumber parties spark delight.
Laughter dances on the breeze,
With fireflies buzzing like little tease.

In this calm, the world unwinds,
Chasing thoughts, oh, what's behind?
With every sigh and snicker loud,
The nighttime echoes, oh so proud.

A Still Heart Under the Stars

Beneath the blanket of the sky,
A sleepy head droops like a tie.
Snores rumble louder than a train,
While raccoons plot mischief in vain.

Pajamas dance in the starlight glow,
As if they're throwing a fashion show.
The moon peeks through a curtain crack,
Caught giggling while shadows sneak back.

Owls wear glasses like sage old men,
Gathering gossip again and again.
Stars listen closely, rolling their eyes,
At the silliness of nocturnal spies.

In this still place, laughter's a thief,
Stealing snores for comic relief.
Each yawn is a tuba's melodic call,
Inviting all to join the ball.

Dreamscapes of the Quiet Night

In the silence of dreams, giggles bloom,
A cat chases shadows in the room.
Pillows whisper secrets to the tides,
As night plays peekaboo with its hides.

In corners, the dust bunnies convene,
Holding meetings, oh so unseen.
They plot against the broom's sharp might,
With schemes that spark in the dead of night.

Beneath the quilt of stars so bright,
An armchair snores, what a funny sight!
Blankets wiggle like they're alive,
Dancing along to a lullaby only they thrive.

As pillows fluff up for a good chat,
They rearrange like a daily spat.
Nighttime's a circus in cozy attire,
Where giggles and dreams never tire.

Lattice of Light and Silence

Within the branches, moonbeams peek,
A turtle shuffles, too cool for a sneak.
Stars flicker old tales like nursery rhymes,
While night watches over the chimes.

Nights full of chuckles are quite the delight,
As shadows take naps, keeping things light.
Crickets patter a tap dance so fine,
Competing with owls who drink moonshine.

A gentle breeze carries cool giggles,
As the world spins quietly, doing its wiggles.
The glow of starry sparkles plays tricks,
As dreams rollercoaster, a wild mix.

Silence hums a tune soft and sweet,
With each breath, a hiccup of beat.
In this gorgeous lattice, laughter swirls,
Molding our nights into twinkling pearls.

Calm Conversations of the Heavens

Stars giggle softly, a wink in the dark,
Planets play hide and seek, oh what a lark.
Moon whispers secrets, a mischievous cheer,
While comets shudder, peeking out near.

Crickets audition, in chirps and in trills,
An owl cracks jokes, spreading nighttime thrills.
Fireflies sparkle, like laughter in flight,
Making the dark just a tad more bright.

Clouds share puns, floating plush and round,
Meteors chuckle, with a whooshing sound.
The universe dances, with rhythm and glee,
In this quirky theater, how funny to be!

So here's to the twilight, a canvas so grand,
With whispers and chuckles, a nighttime band.
Let's laugh with the cosmos till dawn breaks the spell,
For in all this stillness, it's laughter we tell.

Harmony in Nightfall's Embrace

Under the cover of midnight's caress,
Moonlight tiptoes, in sparkly dress.
Bats swoop around, with comical flair,
Claiming the skies, as if they don't care.

A cat on the prowl, a master of stealth,
Knocks over a pot, what a clumsy wealth!
The owl on the tree hoots out a tune,
As laughter erupts, right under the moon.

Stars twinkle gently, like winking eyes,
They share silly jokes, with night's soft sighs.
A breeze rolls through, with whispers that tease,
Ruffling the leaves, like it's meant to please.

Each cool shadow dances, represents cheer,
Finding the funny, in all that we hear.
So hold onto humor, as night wraps around,
In laughter and stillness, true peace can be found.

Starlit Stories Untold

In the quiet of night, the stars begin to chat,
They tell silly tales of a faraway cat.
Frogs jump in with puns, croaking their best,
Each little ribbit, a laugh at the rest.

Comets bringing punchlines, whizzing through the air,
Falling asleep? Dogs would never dare!
With stardust sprinkled over all that's awake,
Night holds a sparkle, for all of our sake.

The moon tries stand-up, it's awkward at best,
While crickets are giggling, not boding a jest.
The trees sway along, doing their dance,
As laughter erupts without any chance.

In this unique theater, where shadows do play,
Even the night sky can brighten your day.
So revel in stories, both silly and bold,
In secret of darkness, are wonders untold.

Evenings Wrapped in Stillness

Blankets of tranquility hug the cool ground,
As shadows make footprints, without a sound.
Grass giggles softly, tickling bare toes,
While night air whispers a joke, who knows?

A raccoon sneezes, starts a laughing fit,
As fireflies flash, adding to the skit.
The moon's soft chuckle, echoes nearby,
With echoes of laughter, it lights up the sky.

Squirrels crack jokes about acorn tales told,
While a distant bat flaps, looking bold.
Each hush holds a giggle, each pause a delight,
As mischief unfolds in the soft, starry night.

So let's raise a smile, to this calm serenade,
In evenings of stillness, where giggles cascade.
Embrace every chuckle, let laughter ignite,
For in silent joys, we find pure delight.

Beneath the Gaze of Stars

Under the sky, a blanket unfurls,
Stars giggle softly like ticklish girls.
Whispers of wind tell silly tales,
Even the moon hides behind its veils.

A cat on the fence, in the middle of a pounce,
Lands on the dog, gives him a bounce.
Noses at war, they dance all around,
While the night's laughter echoes abound.

Crickets throw parties, as they chirp away,
In a language only they can play.
Beetles in tuxedos roll on the ground,
While flowers giggle at the sights they found.

As shadows whisper, the night seems to sway,
With laughter muffled, in a charming ballet.
Underneath this sky, pure silliness reigns,
In the quiet, surprise feasts on our brains.

Crickets' Serenade in Still Hours

Crickets in chorus, a chirp and a laugh,
Making bets on the best grass blade path.
Jumping and jiving, they don't miss a beat,
Under moonbeams, it feels like a treat.

A frog in a top hat, making grand moves,
Practices croaks in slick dance grooves.
While owls roll eyes, with feathers all ruffled,
In this nocturnal show that's beautifully shuffled.

Bees in pajamas buzz off to sleep,
While shadows sneak glances, in secrets they keep.
Night brings a chuckle, in rhythm and rhyme,
When every small creature is up to their crime.

With echoing giggles, the stars light the way,
Frogs leaping high, with nothing to say.
In this quiet laughter, the winds intertwine,
Turning calm nights into pure punchline.

The Mute Dance of Fireflies

Fireflies twinkle, a dazzling parade,
Lights play tag in a glimmering charade.
They flash and they flicker, not one word is spoken,
But giggles and winks, they leave all hearts broken.

In the hush of the night, they zippity-doo,
Drawing shapes in the dark, like a silent zoo.
A spider spins webs, in patterns so fine,
While ants shoplift crumbs, writing their own line.

The breeze starts to chuckle, a soft gentle tease,
As trees dance as if they've had too much freeze.
Beneath this grand stage, the comedy flows,
Where laughter erupts where no one really knows.

With every blink, the fun seems to grow,
In the symphony quiet, where silliness flows.
Even the shadows wear goofy grins,
In the dance of the night, where each tale begins.

The Unspoken Spell of Night

Night's silence speaks in giggles and sighs,
With squirrels plotting, under darkening skies.
Owls share the gossip, with head twirled around,
While grapes sip the moonlight, they tumble to ground.

The dog dreams of chasing a cat on a spree,
In his slumbering antics, he jumps like a flea.
Stars chuckle, and wink, like they've heard the best joke,
While breezes carry laughter, a soft little poke.

Snakes tease the hedgehogs with playful pursuits,
In the dance of the shadows, where mischief roots.
Branches applaud in the softest of tone,
As nighttime's enchantment mercifully shone.

In hushed whispers, secrets begin to arise,
Wrapped up in delight, under starlit skies.
And with every moment, under night's gentle spell,
Silliness sparkles; oh, can you tell?

Secrets of Shadowed Hours

Whispers of the moonlight play,
As socks dance alone in ballet.
The cat plots a midnight raid,
While mice in tuxedos are afraid.

Beneath the stars, secrets unfold,
With tales of fish that once were bold.
The garden gnomes wobble with cheer,
Trading jokes for the world to hear.

In kitchens, spoons start to sway,
Dancing to the fridge's sway.
Cereal boxes join in tune,
Who knew they'd all become a boon?

And as laughter fills the air,
Even shadows join the affair.
These hours, wild and full of mirth,
Are treasures of unmeasured worth.

Midnight's Hidden Laughter

A hiccup from the stars above,
The universe is in love.
Penguins slide on moonbeam trails,
While seahorses tell tall tales.

The clock strikes one, but who will care?
A rabbit tapes its favorite chair.
With hats adorned in ice cream sprinkles,
And purses full of light that twinkles.

Blankets giggle, pillows run,
Chasing dreams, they're having fun.
A dance-off between slippers bold,
Each step a rhythm's story told.

And while the world is fast asleep,
Laughter lingers, secrets keep.
Midnight hums a tune so bright,
In shadows, joy takes flight.

Fantasies in the Dark Embrace

At the stroke of twelve, all's aglow,
Bats wear capes, and on they go.
The night is ripe for sweets and mirth,
Elastic stars bounce with great worth.

Cookies converse in cookie tongues,
Summoning laughs from youngest amongs.
Doughnuts spin in a conga line,
As frosting waves, "This is divine!"

Hiccups echo from stuffed toy bears,
While chaotically floating chairs
Engage in a deep rock-and-roll,
As laughter of shadows fills the hole.

And cats in pajamas strike a pose,
Dancing to music only they know.
In dreams so sweet, the night sways,
With giggles sung in invisible plays.

Luminous Silence

Between the stars, where time may freeze,
Lies a place of giggles and tease.
Dancing shadows, they take a leap,
Making notes of secrets we keep.

Whispers float like cotton candy,
Telling tales of a world less sandy.
Where benches chuckle and trees stand tall,
At daylight's end, they have a ball.

The fridge hums like a cheerful tune,
While forks give cheers to a silver moon.
Curtains sway with flamboyant grace,
As sleepyheads dream in a cozy space.

And laughter sparkles in the air,
With mischief bouncing everywhere.
Luminous dreams light the darkened sky,
As night falls softly with a sigh.

Stars Alight in Solitude

In the hush of darkened skies,
Stars twinkle as if with surprise.
A squirrel leaps, then takes a bow,
Did you see that? I wonder how!

Crickets chirp their nightly tune,
While owls hoot at the silver moon.
A raccoon steals the neighbor's pie,
Oh, what a feast—what a sly guy!

The breeze whispers secrets low,
As shadows dance with no one to show.
Even the cat pretends to stalk,
But trips over a twig—oh, what a walk!

All around, the world is still,
Except for laughter, what a thrill!
Nighttime giggles echo bright,
As mischief thrives in soft moonlight.

A Canvas of Celestial Quiet

Under velvet skies so vast,
Dreams bounce around, they fly so fast.
A toad croaks jokes, all very punny,
While stars giggle—oh, isn't that funny?

The crickets form a nightly band,
Playing symphonies so unplanned.
A firefly joins with a flicker and flash,
As shadows dance and giggles clash.

Clouds drift by, with shapes in tow,
A dragon? A cat? Just go with the flow.
Laughter ripples through the air,
It seems the night loves to share!

While the moon winks, basking in glee,
A satirical tale of the big ol' tree.
With whispers and chuckles, we sip hot tea,
In this celestial theater, how fun it can be!

Serene Echoes of Nightfall

The night unfolds with a cozy sigh,
While I watch a bat zoom by.
Its antics tickle my funny bone,
Returning home—it misses the phone!

Stars play hide and seek so well,
As fog rolls in, an eager swell.
A hedgehog trips, rolls with flair,
To impress a bird, but it's not there!

Mice are plotting their midnight snack,
A crumb or two—they've got the knack.
Laughter bubbles in the quiet land,
With critters creating a wild band.

Even the moon needs a good laugh,
As she tries to draw that silly giraffe.
In this hush, absurdity takes flight,
Each shadow a giggle in the dead of night!

Moonlit Musings

In the glow of the moon's bright face,
Whiskers twitch, a rush of grace.
A cat leaps high, lands like a pro,
Only to slip on a pile of snow!

Owls share stories with raucous glee,
While the stars wink down, can you see?
A bear trying yoga, struck with a pose,
Toppling over—oh, where does it go?

The night is a canvas of quirky fun,
With jokes that dazzle and can't be outdone.
As shadows sway in a whimsical trance,
Who knew twilight could host such a dance?

So here's to the laughter, the chuckles abound,
In the stillness of night, delightful sounds.
Underneath this sparkling sky so dense,
Even silence can crack up—what a sense!

Whispers of the Moonlight

Under the blanket of a starry sky,
Crickets chirp, oh my, oh my!
A cat stares deep into the night,
Chasing shadows, what a fright!

The owls gather to share a laugh,
As raccoons plan a midnight dance.
Who knew that grass could bounce so high?
Oh, vegetables fly by, in a fanciful chance!

With every swoosh, the world is spry,
Squirrels plot to steal a pie.
They giggle as they scurry by,
In their wild, nocturnal spy!

A firefly's glow, a flicker of glee,
Winking softly, just for me.
Silent laughter in the air,
While the world dreams without a care.

Tranquil Embrace of Stars

Underneath the velvet night,
Stars twinkle with a frosty bite.
Fish in ponds wear tiny hats,
While frogs croak jokes about old bats.

The playful breeze begins to tease,
Rustling leaves with perfect ease.
A turtle shuffles, oh so slow,
While giggling shadows put on a show.

Moonbeams bounce off sleepy streams,
Glowworms plot their midnight schemes.
A raccoon laughs at its own joke,
As the evening air begins to cloak.

With pillows made of clouds above,
The world winks, it's got the love.
Hush now, let the silliness rise,
In this realm beneath the skies.

Serenity in Stillness

Under a quilt of gentle night,
Crickets sing with sheer delight.
A squirrel slips on an acorn round,
And the laughter echoes from the ground.

Moonbeams dance, with shadows sleek,
A turtle whispers, "What's next week?"
Breezes tickle the weary trees,
While a cat yawns as it takes aim at bees.

Watch the stars play hide and seek,
While the night hums a quiet tweak.
Owls wearing glasses read their books,
While mice enjoy their midnight looks.

The world is wrapped in a cozy hush,
As the clock gives a gentle rush.
Silent giggles fill the air,
A goofy glow, everywhere!

Echoes of Midnight Calm

In the stillness, a giggle's born,
As the night's magic weaves and's worn.
A lone fox prances, with style to flaunt,
While sleepy leaves whisper and taunt.

The moon beams down, with a cheeky flair,
Bathed in silver, without a care.
A hedgehog quips, "Oh, what a sight!"
As fireflies flicker in pure delight.

A porcupine juggles pine cones bright,
Creating laughter in the pale light.
Raccoons past midnight, oh what a show,
Clumsy little thieves stealing the slow.

Harmony drapes the slumbering ground,
In this scene, joy is easily found.
In the dance of night, what a charm,
With every whisper, all's safe from harm.

Unveiling Dreams in Quiet Spaces

In the stillness, I lie awake,
Hoping a snack will make my heart shake.
The mice have a party, it seems quite right,
Dancing on pillows, till the first light.

Whispers float in the evening air,
Cats plot their takeover, with a feline flair.
Dreams painted in colors of peanut butter,
A world so zany, it makes my heart flutter.

Chasing shadows, the fun never halts,
I giggle at ghosts doing somersaults.
My blanket a fortress, my pillow a throne,
In this wacky kingdom, I am never alone.

So here's to the night, where silliness reigns,
When laughter echoes, and joy never wanes.
Each snicker, each chuckle, a hidden delight,
In the realm of my dreams, all is merry and bright.

The Lull of Hidden Realms

When the clock strikes twelve, my teapot sings,
The kitchen's a circus, where the kettle swings.
Squirrels wear top hats, and rabbits in suits,
High tea in the pantry with whimsical fruits.

In this late hour, mischief's afoot,
The broom serves as wand, in my royal suit.
With cookies for crowns and milk for the cheer,
It's a party of critters, who know no fear.

Lamp light flickers, casting shadows like dancers,
Watch out for the broom, with its funky prancers.
Whirling around, we twirl and we spin,
In this hidden world, we all wear a grin.

So let the quiet stretch, and the giggles arise,
Underneath the moon's glow, we're living the highs.
In the stillness of night, absurdity calls,
We laugh with the moon, till the daylight sprawls.

Tranquility Beneath the Canopy

Beneath the stars, where whispers so soft,
I hear the loud snoring of the dog, oh so loft.
He dreams of great battles, of chasing his tail,
While I sip my cocoa, plans set to unveil.

The trees sing their secrets, a rustling spree,
As critters sneak out for a late-night jubilee.
Acorns are trumpets, the branches their drums,
Tiny concerts commence, with spontaneous hums.

In this tranquil jungle, I giggle with glee,
Imagining elephants taking tea under me.
The owls hold the spotlight, with their wise little eyes,
While hedgehogs in tuxedos practice their sighs.

As the night deepens, so does our spree,
We howl at the moon, let the wildness be free.
In the blanket of darkness, my laughter takes flight,
In this silly habitat, I bask in the night.

Afterglow of Daylight Fading

The sun bows gracefully, ending its show,
While shadows of laughter start to overflow.
Couches transform into ships sailing high,
As I navigate worlds where unicorns fly.

Pajamas are our armor, pillows our shields,
We roam far and wide through imaginary fields.
Bears dance ballet, while the turtles play chess,
In this twilight adventure, there's never a mess.

When bedtime whispers, and yawns start to spread,
I sneak one more cookie, a treat before bed.
In the quiet of corners, giggles ignite,
As dreamers unite in the swell of the night.

So let the darkness wrap us like a warm hug,
With a sprinkle of laughter, and a cozy mug.
For in these soft moments, where worlds intertwine,
The wonders of night are hilariously divine.

The Calm Beyond Dusk

As twilight drapes its gentle cloth,
The moon peeks out with a sly little froth.
Crickets chirp like they just hit a high note,
Even the owls seem to hum, take a note!

Squirrels in pajamas scamper with glee,
Under the stars, they dance wild and free.
A raccoon in a mask, oh what a sight,
Laundry on the line? Nah, it's just night!

Velvet Darkness

The world's snuggled up, tucked in snug tight,
While shadows play tag with pockets of light.
Cats hold their auditions on the rooftops,
While dreamers everywhere just cannot stop!

What fun to let night's silly thoughts roam,
Building pillow forts in every dark home.
With laughter that twinkles like stars in the sky,
Sleep? No way! Who needs it? Oh, my, oh, my!

Whispered Wishes

In the hush of the night where dreams play and tease,
Wishes take flight like a soft, playful breeze.
The toaster's gone rogue, it pops toast in delight,
Every crumb dancing under the moonlight!

Giggling ghosts play cards, what a strange scene,
While the fridge hums a tune like a wobbly machine.
Laughter erupts, as the stars wink away,
Join in the fun—don't let it decay!

Soft Hues of Midnight Reflections

Midnight drapes in colors loud and bright,
Where shadows giggle, oh, what a delight!
An owl tries to hoot but sings like a fool,
Even the trees are now bending the rule.

Each wall tells secrets in whispers and sighs,
While the moon holds court, an owl in disguise.
Gnomes in the garden throw a wild bash,
Marking their territory with a snicker and splash!

Stillness Wrapped in Starlight

Beneath a quilt of glitter, silence abounds,
Where even the pizza delivery guy bounds.
Stars become sprinkles on dark fudgy cake,
And giggles escape like they're trying to wake!

Crickets in tuxedos, they tap dance in sync,
While night air sprinkles stars like a new-jacketed drink.
Let's gather the shadows, bring laughter tonight,
Cuz' everything's better with a sprinkle of light!

Shadows and Softness

The moonlight sneaks through the drapes,
Whispers secrets in soft shapes.
A cat leaps high in silent glee,
Chasing shadows, as wild as can be.

The clock ticks loud, a comical sound,
While snoring echoes, profound and round.
A sock hops by, abandoned and free,
What a ruckus for no one to see!

Each creak of floors makes us giggle,
A ghostly dance, a funny wiggle.
With pillows stacked, our fort is made,
Who knew the night offered such a parade?

Under blankets, we plot to scheme,
In the still, we launch a dream.
With sleepy spells and whispers bright,
Creating mischief in soft twilight.

Laughter in the Silence of Stars

Stars are twinkling; they wink and glow,
Awkwardly silent, our stories flow.
Each giggle echoes, yet no one hears,
The hiccuped laughter disguises our fears.

A comet zooms, then takes a dive,
As teddy bears plot, they come alive.
With nightlights glowing, the games commence,
Whispered truths make little sense!

Fingers freeze, while shadows dance,
Let's surprise the moon with a silly prance.
In this quiet, we rattle and sway,
As if the stars are cheering our play!

Night's gentle breath, a soft embrace,
Swaddled in dreams, we lose our place.
In this hush, we find our spark,
Who knew silence could be so stark?

The Suspended Bliss of Night

In the stillness, a hiccup rings,
Balloons float high with invisible strings.
Whispers of nonsense glide through the air,
Ticklish fingers create wild hair!

A turtle snorts, a frog jumps high,
Jumps on our beds with a curious sigh.
The crickets join in a raucous tune,
A night-time party under a smiling moon.

With giggles suppressed, we count out stars,
Making wishes for candy bars.
In our little world, we laugh and spin,
And wonder when the funny will begin.

With blankets tossed, we leap and bound,
Taking our dreams prancing around.
What a riot in this tranquil space,
For even a whisper can make us race!

Gliding Through the Quiet

In the hush where night crawls slow,
Bunnies parade, putting on a show.
While fireflies dance with a flicker and glow,
A blanket fort hides our giggling flow.

Whispers of mischief bob and weave,
As we plot out a night none will believe.
With ice cream dreams, we tiptoe about,
Too loud we might wake the stars, no doubt!

Each creak of wood is a fun surprise,
A hovercraft dance as a shoe flies high.
In this jubilant calm, we take to flight,
At ease and wild, in the heart of the night.

With grins that stretch from ear to ear,
Sharing our stories, spreading good cheer.
In this soft quilt, let's snicker and play,
Creating laughter in our own special way.

Stars Cradled in Quietude

In the hush, the stars do wink,
As crickets hold a midnight drink.
A raccoon in pajamas prances,
While moonbeams lead the wildest dances.

The owls wear glasses, look quite wise,
As fireflies flash their tiny ties.
The cats hold council, plotting schemes,
In the blanket of night, they chase their dreams.

Reverie Beneath the Stillness

The shadows waltz across the floor,
As laughter echoes at the door.
A cozy brew of dreams in cups,
While sleepy heads just can't give up.

The moon is chuckling at the scene,
Sipping light from a silver sheen.
A bear in slumber writes a song,
While sleepy sighs hum right along.

Echoes of a Peaceful Twilight

The stars are gossiping about the day,
As sleepy clouds drift on their way.
The dog is dreaming of a chase,
While all the stars laugh in their space.

A cozy blanket, a popcorn fight,
Who knew that snoring could sound so bright?
The crickets cheer with every tune,
As night dances with the sleepy moon.

Glistening Dreams in the Dark

Underneath a blanket of glee,
The world slumbers, as cozy as can be.
An old sock puppet tells a tale,
Of knights that ride the backs of snails.

The stars are baking cookies tonight,
With sprinkles that shimmer in the light.
While shadows play hide and seek,
In this charming world, it's blissful and sleek.

A Starlit Pause

Stars twinkle like cheeky sprites,
Whispering secrets in the night.
Crickets tune their tiny fiddles,
While frogs croon their nighttime riddles.

Moonlight sneaks around the trees,
Tickling branches with a breeze.
Squirrels play hide-and-seek with glow,
Their tiny giggles, a sweet show.

Each shadow dances with delight,
A merry prance, a silly sight.
As if the world had gone quite mad,
And merry mischief is the fad.

So let us bask in twilight's cheer,
Where silly antics draw us near.
In the harmony of calm and light,
Every giggle makes this night bright.

Embracing the Calm of Evening

Evening drapes its velvet cloak,
While owls tell the silliest joke.
Rabbits munch on sweet clover,
Exchanging winks, night-time lover.

Fireflies are mood light designers,
Zooming around like tiny miners.
They blink and sway, oh what a show,
Trying to impress, putting on glow.

The gentle breeze holds laughter tight,
As shadows share their funny plight.
A cat trips over her own tail,
Leaving us giggling without fail.

Oh, the wonders of this soothing time,
Where chuckles rise like a rhythm rhyme.
In quiet whispers, humor aligns,
As nature's laughter sweetly shines.

The Symphony of the Unseen

In the stillness, chuckles bloom,
From crickets playing in the gloom.
A raccoon rolls; it's quite a scene,
Creating chaos that's unseen.

Swooping bats like jesters play,
Flipping through shadows on display.
Each flap a giggle, tales in flight,
Spinning stories in the night.

The wind whistles a playful tune,
Softly serenading the moon.
With every rustle, mischief flows,
Every corner chuckles, who knows?

As stars wink down in their disguise,
Listen close to the night's replies.
It's a concert of chuckles, pure and bright,
Unseen revelry fills the night.

Gentle Moans of the Night

Crickets clash in midnight band,
Holding melodies so unplanned.
With every chirp and soft refrain,
They craft a symphony, quite insane.

A sleepy cat lets out a yawn,
Stretching wide as dreams are drawn.
Tails flicker and paws slip,
As night unfolds its funny script.

A breeze whispers jokes through the trees,
Where shadows giggle in soft tease.
The moon, a grinning cheeky lad,
Basks in laughter, feeling glad.

So snuggle up, let your worries fade,
In the dance of night, we're all well-played.
With gentle moans and soft delight,
Life's a comedy in the starlit night.

Milton Keynes UK
Ingram Content Group UK Ltd.
UKHW021846151124
451262UK00014B/1317